SURVIVAL

Leader's Guide

EARTHQUAKE
S U R V I V A L

Leader's Guide

Arlette C. Ballew and Marian K. Prokop

JOSSEY-BASS/PFEIFFER
A Wiley Company
www.pfeiffer.com

Published by

JOSSEY-BASS/PFEIFFER
A Wiley Company
989 Market Street
San Francisco, CA 94103-1741
415.433.1740; Fax 415.433.0499
800.274.4434; Fax 800.569.0443

www.pfeiffer.com

Jossey-Bass/Pfeiffer is a registered trademark of John Wiley & Sons, Inc.

ISBN: 0-88390-450-0

Printed in the United States of America

Printing 10 9 8 7 6 5 4

We at Jossey-Bass strive to use the most environmentally sensitive paper stocks available to us. Our publications are printed on acid-free recycled stock whenever possible, and our paper always meets or exceeds minimum GPO and EPA requirements.

Table of Contents

When To Use Earthquake Survival 1

Administration of Activities 3

    Earthquake Survival Situations (Multiple-Choice Quiz)

    Things To Have in Case of Earthquake (Listing Task)

    Things To Do During and After an Earthquake
       (Listing Task)

Guidelines for Achieving Consensus 9

Synergy 11

Sample Participant Materials 13

    Work Sheets for Activities 15

    Answer Sheets for Activities 27

Further Resources 33

    To Prepare for an Earthquake 33

    During a Major Earthquake 34

    After a Major Earthquake 36

    Home Earthquake Supplies 37

    References and Bibliography 41

When To Use Earthquake Survival

The Purpose of Earthquake Survival[1]

The subject of this simulation (earthquake preparedness and survival) is not the topic for learning. It merely provides an interesting, effective, and entertaining way to introduce the concepts of consensus and synergy in decision making. These concepts are useful to all kinds of problem-solving and decision-making groups in organizations and in other settings. Nonetheless, the information learned about earthquake preparedness and survival may be of great interest and value to many participants.

There are three possible activities in this package. You may use one, two, or all three, depending on your training goals, time available, etc. The administration procedure is the same for all three activities.

Consensus Decision Making

The three activities in this package provide groups and teams with an opportunity to learn how to make decisions by consensus. This may be a new experience for some participants, because many group decisions are made by voting, "trading," or negotiating. In many cases, however, a satisfactory decision can be reached only by consensus. If the members of the group need to feel ownership of a decision in order to abide by it or to implement it, reaching consensus becomes especially important.

---

[1] This package is not intended as an official course in earthquake preparedness and survival.

Synergistic Decision Making

The three activities in this package also explore the concept of synergy with regard to the outcomes of group decision making versus those of individual decision making. They provide firsthand experience in discovering the value of synergistic processes in enhancing both the variety of options considered and the quality of the final decision. They also require the participants to use their interpersonal skills as well as their problem-solving and decision-making skills.

General Problem Solving and Decision Making

In any effort to teach problem-solving or decision-making skills, this package provides an interesting and challenging task for both individuals and the group.

Comparing Individual Decisions with Team Decisions

The activities in this package illustrate the benefits of using all the resources of a team rather than relying solely on the ability of one member to generate ideas or options or to solve a problem or make a decision.

Teamwork

Participants will gain experience in interpersonal behaviors as they work together on the various tasks in this package. They will have opportunities to examine the impacts of their interpersonal behaviors on one another, on the group's effectiveness in accomplishing a task, and on the outcome. In addition, they will have the opportunity to provide one another with supportive and confrontational feedback in a nonthreatening environment.

While observing the group process, the facilitator also will have an opportunity to make notes in order to provide the group as a whole with feedback on its approach to the task, its processes, and its interpersonal dynamics.

Group Behavior

This package provides opportunities to explore many aspects of group behavior in addition to those noted previously. These include: aspects of participation, group member styles, leadership styles, creativity, listening and communication skills, and group self-critique of its functioning.

Administration of Activities

Activity 1:	Earthquake Survival Situations (pages 1 to 4 in *Earthquake Survival Activities.*)
Activity 2:	Things To Have in Case of Earthquake (pages 5 to 7 in *Earthquake Survival Activities.*)
Activity 3:	Things To Do in Case of Earthquake (pages 9 to 11 in *Earthquake Survival Activities.*)
Note:	*All three activities address the same goals and follow the same process.*

Goals

- To allow participants to practice consensus decision making in a task group.

- To provide an opportunity for group members to practice group discussion and decision-making skills.

- To demonstrate the value of synergistic outcomes over individual outcomes.

Group Size

Five to twelve participants. Several subgroups may be directed simultaneously in the same room. (Synergistic outcomes are more likely to be achieved by smaller subgroups, i.e., five to seven participants per subgroup.)

Time Required

Approximately one and one-half hours.

Materials

- A copy of *Earthquake Survival Activities* for each participant.

- A copy of each of the three Earthquake Survival Answer Sheets for each participant.

- A pencil for each participant.

- A portable writing surface (such as a clipboard) for each participant.

- A large copy of the Individual Decisions Tally Sheet (see sample on page 6) on newsprint flip-chart paper or poster paper.

- A large copy of the Group Decisions Tally Sheet (see sample on page 6) on newsprint flip-chart paper or poster paper.

- Blank newsprint flip-chart paper or poster paper.

- Felt-tipped markers.

- Masking tape.

Physical Setting

A room large enough for the entire group to meet and separate rooms or areas in which subgroups can work without distracting one another. Movable chairs should be provided.

Process

1. (*Optional:* Tell the participants that they will be engaging in an individual task and then a subgroup task in order to compare the two activities.) Distribute copies of *Earthquake Survival Activities* to each participant. Tell the participants which of the three individual work sheets to turn to: the Earthquake Survival Situations Individual Work Sheet (page 1), the "Things To Have" Individual Work Sheet (page 5) *or* the "Things To Do" Individual Work Sheet (page 9). Tell the participants that they should work independently on this task. Ask them to read the instructions; when they have done so, tell them to begin the task.

2. After thirteen minutes, give a two-minute warning. After the two minutes, instruct the participants to stop work.

3. Introduce the concept and objectives of consensus decision making. Instruct the participants to turn to page 13 in *Earthquake Survival Activities* and to read the Guidelines for Achieving Consensus. Allow time for them to finish reading the guidelines.

4. Divide the participants into subgroups of four to nine members each, depending on the size of the total group. Tell the participants that each subgroup's task is to reach consensus. Instruct the participants to open their *Earthquake Survival Activities* books to the group work sheet that corresponds to the individual work sheet they completed previously: the Earthquake Survival Situations Group Work Sheet (page 3), the "Things To Have" Group Work Sheet (page 7) *or* the "Things To Do" Group Work Sheet (page 11).

5. Direct the subgroups to separate tables or areas of the room, tell them that they will have thirty minutes in which to reach their consensus decisions, and tell them to begin working.

6. After twenty-five minutes, give a five-minute warning. Then give a two-minute warning. When the time is up, instruct the subgroups to stop working and to reassemble, bringing their work sheets with them.

7. Give a copy of the appropriate answer sheet to each participant. *[Note: The answer sheets are color keyed: the Earthquake Survival Situations Answer Sheet is teal, the "Things To Have" Answer Sheet is pink, and the "Things To Do" Answer Sheet is yellow.]* Read the answers aloud or allow participants to read the answers themselves.

8. Post the large copy of the Individual Decisions Tally Sheet (see page 6). Have each participant compare his or her *individual scores* to the "correct" answers. Ask participants to report how many "right" answers they had and record these on the tally sheet. For each subgroup, draw a circle around the number of correct answers for the *highest scorer* in the group. Then compute the *average* number of correct answers for the individuals in each subgroup. *[Note: The average is computed by adding the individual scores of all subgroup members and dividing by the number of subgroup members.]*

9. Now post a large copy of the Group Decisions Tally Sheet (see page 6) and ask the groups to report, from the lists generated by consensus, how many "right" answers they had. Record these in the "Subgroup Score" column. Now copy the highest individual score for each subgroup and the average score for each subgroup (from the Individual Decisions Tally Sheet) and enter them to the right of the subgroup's score. Compare the numbers and enter a plus or minus and a number to indicate whether the highest and average individual scores for each subgroup are higher or lower than the subgroup's score and what the numerical difference is.

10. Remind the participants that the goal was not to test their knowledge of earthquake preparedness; it was to allow them to explore the process of reaching group consensus.

11. Introduce the concept of synergy (you may wish to use the lecturette on page 11 of this Leader's Guide). Ask how the comparison of the individual scores with the subgroups' scores supports or refutes this concept. For each

Individual Decisions Tally Sheet

Name of Subgroup Member	Number of Correct Items			
	Subgroup 1	Subgroup 2	Subgroup 3	Subgroup 4
Example: Member x	8	10	9	12
Subgroup Total				
Subgroup Average*				

*Subgroup Average is calculated by dividing the Subgroup Total by the number of subgroup members.

Group Decisions Tally Sheet

Subgroup	Subgroup Score	Highest Individual Score (+/-)	Average Individual Score (+/-)	Synergy?
Example: Subgroup x	14	10 (-4)	8 (-6)	Yes
Subgroup 1				
Subgroup 2				
Subgroup 3				
Subgroup 4				

subgroup, note on the Group Decisions Tally Sheet whether or not the subgroup score seems to indicate a synergistic outcome (as shown in the sample).

12. Use the following questions to guide the participants in a discussion of the activity:

- What behaviors helped the consensus-seeking process?

- What behaviors hindered the consensus-seeking process?

- What patterns of decision making occurred?

- Were some group members more influential than others? How did this happen?

- Did the group discover and use all its information resources? If so, how did it do this? If not, why not?

- For the groups that experienced synergy, what else happened during their deliberations that facilitated a synergistic outcome?

- For any groups that did not experience synergy, what happened during their deliberations that might have inhibited synergy?

- In what kinds of situations would consensus decision making be most appropriate?

- In what situations might consensus decision making be inappropriate?

- What are the implications of consensus seeking and synergistic outcomes for task groups such as work groups, committees, staff groups, and so on?

13. If desired to reinforce the learnings or to provide additional skill practice, this activity may be repeated using work sheets that were not used in the first round and the corresponding answer sheet.

[Optional: After you have completed all the activities that you will be using from this package, duplicate and distribute the information found in the "Further Resources" section at the end of this Leader's Guide. It contains more comprehensive information about earthquake preparedness and survival, much of which is not included on the participants' answer sheets.]

Variations

- Sequential consensus exercises can be used, so that subgroups build on what was learned in the first phase. New subgroups can be formed for the second round.

- Process observers can be used to provide feedback about group behavior or individual and group behavior. Behaviors to note include the following:

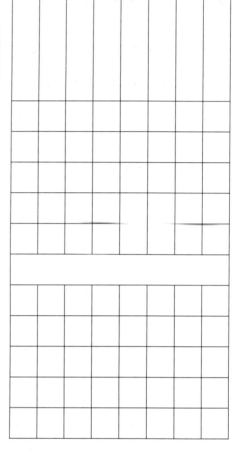

+Behaviors

Suggesting procedures, sharing leadership

Showing enthusiasm

Encouraging others to participate

Helping team to assess its performance

Praising or supporting others

- Behaviors

Acting withdrawn or unwilling to participate

Getting angry or sulking

Showing off, seeking individual attention

Disrupting or disturbing team process

Criticizing or ridiculing others

- The group-on-group design can be used to heighten participation for consensus seeking. Two rounds can be used, with two different tasks.

- Participants can be asked to rank order one another (independently) in terms of the amount of influence each had on the consensus-seeking outcomes. Then each participant derives a score for himself or herself based on the differences between self-ranking of the items and the consensus ranking. The average influence ranks and the differences scores are then correlated.

Guidelines for Achieving Consensus

Consensus is a method of reaching agreement in problem-solving and decision-making groups in which all the parties involved actively discuss the issues surrounding the decision, thus incorporating the knowledge and experience, ideas and feelings of all members. In the sense that it is used in this activity, reaching consensus means that all members of the group reach substantial agreement (i.e., everyone agrees to some extent) that they can live with the decision, ranking, etc. Because any final decision must be supported to some degree by each member of the group, all members work together on a mutually acceptable solution, rather than producing a "we-they" situation.

As you might imagine, decision by consensus may be difficult to attain and may consume more time than other methods of decision making. The energies of the group become focused on the problem at hand (rather than on defending individual points of view). This approach to problem solving and decision making often results in a higher-quality decision than do other methods such as the use of majority power (voting), minority power (persuasion), and compromise. Although these are often easier methods of decision making, they may not include a careful weighing of all the relevant information. A major result of achieving consensus is that no member feels violated or ignored, and commitment to the agreement is stronger as a result.

In the consensus-seeking process, you are asked to do the following:

Prepare your own position as well as possible prior to meeting with the group (but realize that the task is incomplete and that missing pieces will be supplied by other members of the group).

Express your own opinion and explain it fully, so that the rest of the group has the benefit of all members' thinking.

Listen to the opinions and feelings of all other group members and be ready to modify your own position on the basis of logic and understanding.

Avoid arguing in order to win as an individual; what is "right" is the best collective judgment of the group as a whole.

View disagreements or conflict about ideas, solutions, etc., as helping to clarify the issue rather than as hindering the process of seeking consensus. Do not "give in" if you still have serious reservations about an issue; instead, work toward resolution.

Recognize that tension-reducing behaviors, such as laughing, kidding, making comments, and so on, can be useful so long as meaningful conflict is not "smoothed over" prematurely.

Refrain from conflict-reducing techniques such as voting, averging, trading, compromising, or giving in to keep the peace.

Monitor the interactions between people as well as what is done as the group attempts to complete its work and initiate discussions of what really is going on.

The best results flow from a fusion of information, logic, and emotion. Consensus seeking offers the promise of marshalling group resources to produce synergistic outcomes without denying the integrity of individual members.

Synergy

Synergy is "the combined action of two or more agents that, acting jointly, increase the effectiveness of one another and produce an outcome that is greater than the sum of their outcomes when acting independently." Synergy can be expected when the members of a group work together on a consensus-seeking task. The combined knowledge, judgment, and problem-solving and decision-making abilities of the members generally produce a score that is higher (i.e., more "correct" answers) than the average individual score. However, the fact that several people are meeting together and producing a solution does not necessarily mean that all their abilities will be utilized. Synergy is more likely to occur when the subgroup follows the Guidelines for Achieving Consensus.

If members have no common goal, if each strives to be "number one" and to have his or her ideas accepted over others, and if members adopt a competitive "win-lose" mentality, it is likely that the group's outcome will be less than effective or desirable. However, if group members approach a task in a mutual, problem-solving manner, the remark that "two heads are better than one" is usually validated. When people work together collaboratively, a synergistic effect often develops and the group's results exceeds the sum of the contributions of the individuals.

The concept of group synergy means looking at outcomes in a noncompetitive way. It requires breaking out of a dysfunctional "either-or" mentality and creating a functional type of competition (i.e., stimulation). Winning becomes a group effort rather than an individual quest. Conflict is viewed as an asset rather than as something to be avoided. The members look for bridges between ideas, for wholes rather than parts. Collaboration in generating ideas, planning, and problem solving creates consensual validation of individuals' points of view and sparks more ideas.

Work groups achieve synergy when the process of working heightens sharing and contributing. When members truly listen to one another, share ideas and opinions, stay on the topic, and attend to group process, they are more likely to achieve synergy. In a consensus task, the possibility of synergy is increased because the group reaches substantial agreement rather than splitting into majority and minority camps.

However, it is likely that a group will not produce a synergistic score if members of that group carry on more than one conversation at a time, interrupt one another, jump from one subject to another, and/or allow some members not to participate. To enjoy synergy, the group members must not only work toward producing the best solution, but they must also pay close attention to the process they are using to reach the solution.

What energy is to the individual, synergy is to the group. The synergy of a group always is potentially greater than the sum of the combined energies of its members. The group effort often produces better results than the group's most competent member could have achieved alone. Effective work teams not only use their energy effectively, they create new energy.

Sample Participant Materials

Earthquake Survival Situations Individual Work Sheet 15

Earthquake Survival Situations Group Work Sheet 17

"Things To Have" Individual Work Sheet 19

"Things To Have" Group Work Sheet 21

"Things To Do" Individual Work Sheet 23

"Things To Do" Group Work Sheet 25

Earthquake Survival Situations Answer Sheet 27

"Things To Have" Answer Sheet 29

"Things To Do" Answer Sheet 31

Earthquake Survival Situations Individual Work Sheet

Instructions: Following are twelve questions concerning personal survival in an earthquake situation. Your task is individually to select the best of the three options given under each item. Do not communicate with anyone as you work on this task. Try to imagine yourself in the situation depicted. Assume that you are alone and have a minimum of equipment, except where specified. The season is fall. The days are warm and dry, but the nights are cold.

_____ 1. What appliance in your home presents the greatest danger to you during an earthquake?

    a. Refrigerator.

    b. Water heater.

    c. Gas stove.

_____ 2. On average, how many earthquakes per year are felt in California?

    a. 100.

    b. 2400.

    c. 5000.

_____ 3. On average, how long does it take relief efforts to reach a neighborhood after a major disaster?

    a. 24 hours.

    b. 3 days.

    c. 5 days.

_____ 4. Which of the following is the weakest structure of most homes?

    a. Roof.

    b. Foundation.

    c. Porches/patios.

_____ 5. In the years between 1989 and 1993, how many people in the United States were killed in earthquakes?

    a. 180.

    b. 302.

    c. 68.

_____ 6. A tsunami is a

     a. wind condition that precedes an earthquake.

     b. tidal wave.

     c. fissure in the ground as a result of an earthquake.

_____ 7. How many of the 50 United States are earthquake prone?

     a. 39.

     b. 11.

     c. 27.

_____ 8. If you are in a car when an earthquake strikes, you should *not*

     a. stay in the car.

     b. pull off the road, away from anything that could fall on the car.

     c. leave your car and start walking for shelter.

_____ 9. If you are in a building when an earthquake strikes, you should *not*

     a. leave the building in case it collapses.

     b. crawl under a sturdy table or desk.

     c. brace yourself against the walls of an interior hallway.

_____ 10. Which source of drinking water should be your last resort?

     a. Water from the water heater.

     b. Water from the flush tank of a toilet.

     c. Water from a swimming pool.

_____ 11. Which of the following is least important to keep next to your bed in case of earthquakes?

     a. Flashlight.

     b. Bottled water.

     c. Bicycle helmet.

_____ 12. If family members are separated after an earthquake, each should call

     a. a family member who lives nearby.

     b. a friend or relative outside of town.

     c. the local police department.

Earthquake Survival Situations Group Work Sheet

Instructions: Following are twelve questions concerning personal survival in an earthquake situation. Your subgroup's task is to decide, by consensus, the best answer for each question. (Again, assume that in the earthquake situation you are alone and have a minimum of equipment, except where specified. The season is fall. The days are warm and dry, but the nights are cold.)

Note: Do not change your individual answers, even if you change your mind during the subgroup discussion. Both the individual and subgroup solutions will later be compared with answers recommended by earthquake survival experts.

_____ 1. What appliance in your home presents the greatest danger to you during an earthquake?

   a. Refrigerator.

   b. Water heater.

   c. Gas stove.

_____ 2. On average, how many earthquakes per year are felt in California?

   a. 100.

   b. 2400.

   c. 5000.

_____ 3. On average, how long does it take relief efforts to reach a neighborhood after a major disaster?

   a. 24 hours.

   b. 3 days.

   c. 5 days.

_____ 4. Which of the following is the weakest structure of most homes?

   a. Roof.

   b. Foundation.

   c. Porches/patios.

_____ 5. In the years between 1989 and 1993, how many people in the United States were killed in earthquakes?

   a. 180.

   b. 302.

   c. 68.

_____ 6. A tsunami is a

    a. wind condition that precedes an earthquake.

    b. tidal wave.

    c. fissure in the ground as a result of an earthquake.

_____ 7. How many of the 50 United States are earthquake prone?

    a. 39.

    b. 11.

    c. 27.

_____ 8. If you are in a car when an earthquake strikes, you should _not_

    a. stay in the car.

    b. pull off the road, away from anything that could fall on the car.

    c. leave your car and start walking for shelter.

_____ 9. If you are in a building when an earthquake strikes, you should _not_

    a. leave the building in case it collapses.

    b. crawl under a sturdy table or desk.

    c. brace yourself against the walls of an interior hallway.

_____ 10. Which source of drinking water should be your last resort?

    a. Water from the water heater.

    b. Water from the flush tank of a toilet.

    c. Water from a swimming pool.

_____ 11. Which of the following is least important to keep next to your bed in case of earthquakes?

    a. Flashlight.

    b. Bottled water.

    c. Bicycle helmet.

_____ 12. If family members are separated after an earthquake, each should call

    a. a family member who lives nearby.

    b. a friend or relative outside of town.

    c. the local police department.

Earthquake Survival "Things To Have" Individual Work Sheet

Instructions: As you work individually on this task, do not communicate with anyone. Your task is to create a list of fifteen *items* that are most needed in case of a major earthquake. These may be items that you would want to have in your home, office, or automobile. The priority among the fifteen items is not important, but they should be the fifteen items *that you would need most* in case of an earthquake disaster.

1. _____

2. _____

3. _____

4. _____

5. _____

6. _____

7. _____

8. _____

9. _____

10. _____

11. _____

12. _____

13. _____

14. _____

15. _____

Earthquake Survival "Things To Have" Group Work Sheet

You have just created an individual list of things to have in case of an earthquake. Now your subgroup will create a list by consensus. Remember, reaching a decision by consensus is difficult, and not every decision may meet with everyone's unqualified approval. There should be, however, a general feeling of support from all members before a subgroup decision is made. Try to follow the Guidelines for Achieving Consensus as you work on this task.

Instructions: Your subgroup's task is to create *one* list of fifteen items that are most needed in case of a major earthquake. The priority among the fifteen items is not important, but they should be the fifteen items *that your subgroup agrees you would need most* in case of an earthquake disaster.

1. _____

2. _____

3. _____

4. _____

5. _____

6. _____

7. _____

8. _____

9. _____

10. _____

11. _____

12. _____

13. _____

14. _____

15. _____

Earthquake Survival "Things To Do" Individual Work Sheet

Instructions: As you work individually on this task, do not communicate with anyone. Your task is to create a list of fifteen *things that are most important to do or not do during and immediately after* a major earthquake. Assume that you will be at home when the earthquake occurs. You may want to think about what you would do first, what you would do next, etc., but do not worry about prioritizing. The most important thing is to get fifteen things written down.

1. _____

2. _____

3. _____

4. _____

5. _____

6. _____

7. _____

8. _____

9. _____

10. _____

11. _____

12. _____

13. _____

14. _____

15. _____

Earthquake Survival "Things To Do" Group Work Sheet

You have just created an individual list of things to do or not to do during and immediately after an earthquake. Now your subgroup will create a list by consensus. Remember, reaching a decision by consensus is difficult, and not every decision may meet with everyone's unqualified approval. There should be, however, a general feeling of support from all members before a subgroup decision is made. Try to follow the Guidelines for Achieving Consensus as you work on this task.

Instructions: Your subgroup's task is to create *one* list of the fifteen things that are most important to do or not do in case of a major earthquake. The priority among the fifteen actions is not important, but they should be the fifteen things *that your subgroup agrees you should or should not do* in case of an earthquake disaster.

1. _____
2. _____
3. _____
4. _____
5. _____
6. _____
7. _____
8. _____
9. _____
10. _____
11. _____
12. _____
13. _____
14. _____
15. _____

EARTHQUAKE SURVIVAL
Earthquake Survival Situations
Answer Sheet

Arlette C. Ballew and Marian K. Prokop

Following are the answers to each of the questions on the Earthquake Survival Situations Work Sheet. These responses are considered to be the most correct for most situations; specific situations, however, might require other courses of action.

1. (b) Because they are so top heavy, water heaters are likely to fall over during an earthquake, possibly rupturing the gas line, and causing water and fire damage.

2. (c) It is estimated that residents of California experience an average of 5000 earthquakes each year.

3. (b) Experience has shown that it takes an average of three days for relief supplies to reach a neighborhood.

4. (c) Because many porches or patios are added after a building is constructed, they are most likely to collapse in an earthquake and could block exits.

5. (c) Only 68 people died from earthquakes in the United States between 1989 and 1993.

6. (b) A tsunami (tsoo nä me) is an unusually large tidal wave produced by an undersea volcanic eruption or earthquake.

7. (a) Thirty-nine states in the United States are earthquake prone.

8. (c) You should not leave your car. A car gives you a relatively safe place to wait out the tremors; your car radio is a potential source of information about your options.

9. (a) You should not leave the building. Stairways may be damaged, and debris is most likely to fall just outside of exits. Bracing yourself against the walls of an interior hallway is the action most recommended. An interior doorway offers structural protection, but a door may be slammed against you during the tremor. Crawling under a sturdy table or desk will afford air space and protection from falling objects.

10. (c) Water from a swimming pool is chlorinated and can cause diarrhea and kidney damage if used for drinking. Water from a swimming pool is, however, safe to use for bathing and sanitary needs.

11. (b) Bottled water is not as important as the other items. You will need to put on shoes to prevent injuries from broken glass; you will need the flashlight in case the electricity is not in service; and the bicycle helmet can protect you from falling objects. Presumably you have a store of bottled water elsewhere in your home as part of your earthquake-preparedness supplies.

12. (b) Call a friend or relative who lives outside of town. That person can serve as a "message center" and relay messages to other friends and family members. This leaves the telephone lines in the quake area open for emergencies.

EARTHQUAKE SURVIVAL
"Things To Have" Answer Sheet

Arlette C. Ballew and Marian K. Prokop

The following is a list of the twenty-five items that most experts agree are most important to have in an accessible place in the event of a major earthquake. These supplies (except for the last one) may be stored in sturdy plastic containers (such as trash cans).

Note: If you live in an area that is earthquake prone, take steps immediately to obtain and store these supplies. Experience shows that the longer you wait, the less likely you are to prepare.

1. Water (for each person and pet for 3 days—2 gallons per person per day)

2. Food (for each person and pet for a minimum of 3 days—dried/canned)

3. Extra eyeglasses

4. Required prescription medicines and other personal medical supplies (keep list of expiration dates)

5. First aid kit (a good one) and handbook

6. Large, resealable plastic bags for human refuse and for daily garbage (food, sanitary, bandages, etc.)

7. Toilet tissue

8. Basic personal-hygiene items, including special items for babies, elderly persons, and pets

9. Flashlight and extra batteries

10. Shortwave radio/battery-operated radio

11. Plastic sheets/tarps

12. Thermal blankets/blankets

13. Cash (including coins for telephones)

14. Change of clothes (per person)

15. Hard shoes and socks (per person)

Your leader has more complete information on how to prepare and what to have on hand.

16. Candles and matches in waterproof container

17. Mechanical can opener (if food is canned)

18. Work gloves

19. Duct tape

20. Crowbar

21. Note pad and pens/pencils

22. Emergency phone numbers (including number of a contact person who lives outside your area)

23. Extra set of car keys

24. Plastic cups, utensils, etc.

25. Fireproof box with important papers (including full names and Social Security number of all members of family, photographs of family members and pets, vehicle ID numbers and license numbers, insurance policies, charge account numbers, video of valuables/contents of house, etc.)

EARTHQUAKE SURVIVAL
"Things To Do" Answer Sheet

Arlette C. Ballew and Marian K. Prokop

The following is a list of the twenty-five things that most experts agree are most important to do or not do during and immediately after a major earthquake.

Note: If you live in an area that is earthquake prone, take steps immediately to do these things. Experience shows that the longer you wait, the less likely you are to prepare.

1. Stay put, protect your head and face, and brace yourself from being thrown around.

2. If you can do so quickly and safely enough, duck under a table or sturdy desk that will provide you with cover and air space and hang on to it. If the furniture moves, hold on and move with it.

3. Another option during an earthquake is to brace yourself against the walls of an inner hallway without bookcases, glass on the walls, or things that could break or fly. Put your back against one wall and your feet against the other to stabilize yourself.

4. A third option during an earthquake is to brace yourself in a supported doorway, away from things that could fall on you or break.

5. If you are in a safe area, stay there! Do not attempt to use stairs or elevators. If you are inside, do not attempt to go outside. There are numerous dangers in doing so, including falling debris, damaged stairways or exits, power outages in elevators or stairwells, and trampling or other injury by panicked people.

6. If you are outside, stay there. Move away from high buildings, walls, power lines and poles, lamp posts, etc. Watch for fallen power lines. If possible, proceed cautiously to an open area.

7. Use a flashlight. Do not turn on a light switch. Do not light a match, fire, gas stove, etc., until you are sure there is no danger of gas leakage. Be sure to relight any pilot lights when gas service is restored.

8. Put on sturdy shoes to protect yourself from broken glass, etc. If there is debris, put on sturdy gloves and a dust mask, too. A hard hat/blanket/coat/cardboard will help to protect your head from further falling objects.

9. Check for injuries; administer first aid.

Your leader has more complete information on what to do and what not to do.

10. Check for fires, gas leaks, water leaks, chemical leaks, etc.

11. Check utilities. Shut off water and gas lines if advisable. Shut off the electricity if necessary and unplug electrical appliances.

12. Collect a moderate amount of cold water from tap if possible and save it.

13. Put telephone receivers back on their cradles, to help the telephone company deal with the overload. Do not use the telephone except in true emergency. Leave the lines open for emergeny agencies. If family members are separated, call only your out-of-area contact. Others can call this person for information. Tell this person if you plan to evacuate. Unplug your phones at the wall if you are leaving the area.

14. Turn on a battery-operated radio (or short-wave radio or car radio) and listen for emergency bulletins and instructions.

15. Open doors, cupboards, and closets carefully, checking for structural damage, debris, and falling objects.

16. Clean up hazardous materials. Use work gloves/plastic gloves, hard hats—such as bicycle helmets—and dust masks if needed.

17. Take routine medications.

18. Confine frightened pets.

19. Check that sewer lines are intact before flushing any toilets. Plug tub and sink drains to prevent sewage backup.

20. Do not go without food or water for too long, as this will weaken you.

21. Check for structural damage; evacuate if necessary.

22. Expect and prepare for aftershocks. Check chimneys and other areas that may be unstable and keep people and things away from them.

23. Take mirrors, pictures, china, etc., off walls and put them where they are not hazards.

24. Respond to requests from local officials, police, firefighters, and emergency-relief organizations.

25. Stay in a safe area. Do not drive; leave the streets clear for emergency vehicles. Avoid downed power lines; do not go near damaged structures; do not go near possible landslide areas; do not go near the beach, because of the danger of tsunamis.

Further Resources

To Prepare for an Earthquake

1. Check water and gas shutoffs; make sure everyone knows where they are and how to use them.

2. Grease pipe/crescent wrenches for gas and water shutoff valves and put the wrenches in sealed plastic bags accessible to the shutoff valves.

3. Have a shake-turnoff valve installed on the gas line.

4. Know how to turn off the electricity.

5. Strap the water heater to the wall or otherwise secure it.

6. Purchase fire extinguishers (ABC) and place them in strategic locations. Teach family members how to use them. Clean up any fire hazards around your home, garage, and yard. Install smoke detectors and check their batteries regularly.

7. Put flex hose on gas connections on the water heater, dryer, and stove.

8. Arrange with a neighbor to turn off your water and gas and to take care of children/elderly family member/pets in case you are not at home. Give the neighbor signed authorization forms and signed medical release forms for each person/pet. Arrange any other support plans with neighbor(s).

9. Register your pet and put the license tag on its collar.

10. Put latches on cabinet doors.

11. Secure stereo components, computer components, telephones, etc., with Velcro™ pads or straps.

12. Secure cabinets, bookcases, entertainment centers, etc., to walls with "L" brackets or by other means.

13. Secure pictures, mirrors, hanging shelves, clocks, etc., to walls with closed-hook hangers or special screw braces at bottoms of frames.

14. Put hard shoes and bicycle helmets under beds.

15. Keep dust masks and flashlights in bedside storage areas.

16. Move beds away from windows, hanging mirrors or pictures, and other objects that could shatter or topple.

17. Keep family immunizations up to date.

18. Prepare an earthquake survival kit and store the items in plastic container(s) in a sheltered area inside house (closets on interior walls work well) or in large plastic trashcan(s) in a secure area in the yard (see list that follows). Check freshness of supplies every six months.

19. Prepare mini-survival kits for the office and automobiles. Prepare an evacuation kit for the family. (See lists that follow.)

20. Change medications/food/water in kits at appropriate intervals.

21. Identify hazardous areas in your home and office (windows, glass doors, shower doors, mirrors, large glass-fronted pictures, fireplaces, unreinforced brick/masonry walls, bookcases, china cabinets, stacked stereo/media units, tall furniture, etc.).

22. Designate an out-of-area contact person who will receive telephone calls and relay messages among family members and friends if telephone lines in your area are affected. Tell this person your overall plan and where family members plan to meet eventually if they are separated because of an earthquake.

23. Train children and other household members what to do during and after an earthquake (including what to do in case of fire, where emergency supplies are stored, the number of the out-of-area contact person, where to meet eventually if you are separated, etc.).

24. Keep the gas tank of your automobile filled with fuel.

25. Check your earthquake insurance for fire, fire from an outside force or neighbor's house, flood, and aftershock.

26. If your home has multiple floors, have a portable fire-escape ladder near the most likely "emergency exit" window.

27. Have your home inspected to determine if the foundation is bolted to the sill plate, the cripple walls are reinforced, etc. If necessary, have your home structurally reinforced by a professional.

During a Major Earthquake

1. Call to children to remain calm and do what they have been trained to do.

2. In many cases, it is not wise to attempt to move during an earthquake. If you have time and can move safely, choose the nearest safe area that will

provide cover and air space if the building collapses (e.g., under a table, an inner hallway). Hold on to something secure if you can, if not, try to stabilize yourself so you will not be thrown around.

If you are indoors, the nearest safe area may be one of the following:

- Under a sturdy table or desk. (Hold on to a support to stabilize yourself from moving. If the furniture moves, move with it, hanging on.)

- A inner hallway without bookcases, glass on walls, or things that could break/fly. (Sit with your back against one wall, with your feet wedged against other wall to stabilize you from moving.)

- In bed. (It may be best to stay there, protecting your head and face. If the bed is sturdy and there is room, you may get under the bed.)

- An inside corner, away from windows. (Sit and brace yourself as best you can.)

- A supported doorway—not as good as a sturdy table/desk or safe hallway. (Assume same position as for a hallway.) Be careful of being hit if a door slams.

- A supported inside wall. (The inner core of a building is usually the strongest and least likely to collapse.)

3. Protect your head and face. If you are not under cover, you may be able to grab a coat, blanket, newspapers, box, etc., to protect your head and face from shattered glass or falling objects.

4. If you are in the shower or bathtub, drop to the bottom. Turn off the water. Assume a position that will best keep you from slipping and cover your head, face, and neck with a towel, shower curtain, or your hands. Look for broken glass, tiles, and mirrors before moving.

5. Do not attempt to go up or down stairs or use elevators! If you are inside, do not attempt to go outside. There are numerous dangers in doing this, among which are falling debris, broken stairways or exits, power outages in elevators or stairwells, and trampling or other injury by panicked people.

6. If you are outside, stay there. Move away from high buildings, walls, power lines and poles, lamp posts, etc. Watch for fallen power lines. If possible, proceed cautiously to an open area.

7. If you are in a moving automobile, stop as quickly as you safely can, but try not to stop on a highway overpass or bridge that might collapse. Do not stop where an overpass, bridge, or building could fall on you. Stay in the car; it is a relatively safe "shock absorber." If an electrical wire falls on your car, remain in the car, which probably is well insulated and will protect you unless you touch charged metal.

After a Major Earthquake

1. Do not light a match or turn on an electrical switch; use a flashlight.

2. Put on sturdy shoes to protect yourself from broken glass, etc. If there is debris, put on sturdy gloves and a dust mask, too. A hard hat/bicycle helmet/blanket/coat/cardboard will help to protect your head from further falling objects.

3. Check for injuries; administer first aid.

4. Check for fires, gas leaks, water leaks, chemical leaks, etc.

5. Check utilities. Shut off water and gas lines if advisable. Shut off the electricity if necessary and unplug electrical appliances. (Do not turn main switches back on until they have been properly inspected.)

6. Check tap water. If clear, collect a *moderate* amount of cold water and save it. (Later water may be contaminated.)

7. Put any telephone receivers back on their cradles, to help the telephone company to deal with the overloaded system. Do not attempt to use the telephone except in true emergency. Leave the lines open for emergency agencies. Unplug your phone lines at the wall if you are leaving the area.

8. Turn on a battery-operated radio (or short-wave radio or car radio) and listen for emergency bulletins and instructions.

9. Clean up hazardous materials. (Use work gloves/plastic gloves, hard hats—such as bicycle helmets—and dust masks if needed. You may want to take "after the quake" photos, if possible, to document damage for IRS and insurance claims.)

10. Take routine medications.

11. Confine frightened pets. (Many pets are lost or injured after natural disasters.)

12. Check that sewer lines are intact before flushing any toilets. Plug bathtub and sink drains to prevent sewage backup.

13. Do not go without food or water for too long, as this will weaken you.

14. Do not eat/drink from open containers; they may contain shattered glass or other debris. If possible, use food from the refrigerator the first day. Frozen food should keep for three days in an unopened freezer.

15. Do not light matches, fires, gas stove, etc., if there is danger of gas leakage.

16. Check the building for structural damage; evacuate if necessary. (See list for "evacuation kit" that follows.)

17. Open cupboards and closet doors carefully and watch for falling objects.

18. If safe, check to see if neighbor's children/elderly family member/pets are alone/uncared for.

19. Expect and prepare for aftershocks. Check chimneys and other areas that may be unstable and keep people and things away from them. Protect valuable furniture by covering it with blankets or newspapers and cardboard. Take mirrors, pictures, china, etc., off walls and put them where they are not hazards.

20. Secure your home as best as possible if windows are broken, doors are jammed open, etc. Be careful that you do not incur further structural damage in doing so.

21. Respond to requests from local officials, police, firefighters, and emergency-relief organizations.

22. Stay away from dangerous areas (e.g., avoid downed power lines; do not go near damaged structures; do not go near possible landslide areas; do not go near the beach, because of the danger of tsunamis.) Do not go "sightseeing."

23. Do not drive unless absolutely necessary. Leave the streets clear for emergency vehicles.

24. Find safe, appropriate tasks for children and other family members to do in order to help them to cope.

25. Be extra careful about sanitation. Keep hands and fingers out of mouths.

26. If telephone service is available but limited, call only your out-of-area contact person. Other family members and friends can call this person to find out how you are and exchange information about others. Tell this person if you plan to evacuate.

27. Be sure to relight any pilot lights when the gas service is restored.

Home Earthquake Supplies

To Keep in Sturdy Plastic Containers or Trash Cans

*Minimum*_____

- [ ] Water (for each person and pet for 3 days—2 gallons per person per day)
- [ ] Food (for each person and pet for a minimum of 3 days—dried/canned/emergency food bars/military ration packs)
- [ ] Extra prescription eyeglasses
- [ ] Required prescription medicines and other personal medical supplies (keep list of expiration dates)
- [ ] Cash (including coins for telephones)

- [ ] Resealable plastic bags for human refuse
- [ ] Resealable plastic bags for daily garbage (food, sanitary, bandages, etc.)
- [ ] Toilet tissue
- [ ] Basic personal-hygiene items (premoistened towelettes, toothbrushes and toothpaste, deodorant, comb, soap, shampoo, sanitary napkins, etc.)
- [ ] Special items for babies or elderly persons
- [ ] Large plastic trash bags for accumulated trash, with ties to close them
- [ ] First aid kit (a complete one, including gauze bandages, surgical tape, scissors, antiseptic, antibiotic ointment, aspirin/buffered aspirin, etc.) and handbook
- [ ] Flashlight and extra batteries
- [ ] Shortwave radio/battery-operated radio
- [ ] Plastic sheets/tarps
- [ ] Thermal blankets/blankets
- [ ] Change of clothes (per person)

- [ ] Hard shoes and socks (per person)
- [ ] Jacket (per person)
- [ ] Candles (wide-based candles do not require candlesticks)
- [ ] Matches in a waterproof container
- [ ] Mechanical can opener (if food is canned)
- [ ] Pet dish
- [ ] Plastic cups, plastic utensils, plastic dishes
- [ ] Work gloves
- [ ] Dust filter masks
- [ ] Cord/rope
- [ ] Duct tape
- [ ] Crowbar
- [ ] Dog leash, cat carrier
- [ ] Note pad and pens/pencils
- [ ] Authorization to take care of neighbors' children/elderly family members/pets
- [ ] Emergency phone numbers (including number of out-of-area contact person)
- [ ] An extra set of car keys

Also Recommended

- [ ] Portable toilet and disposable liner bags
- [ ] Water-purification tablets such as Halazone and globaline (be sure to read the label on the bottle before using) or liquid chlorine bleach (16 drops per gallon of water; let stand for $\frac{1}{2}$ hour)

- [ ] Household disinfectant/powdered chlorinated lime (the latter not available in some states)
- [ ] Sunblock
- [ ] Boy Scout Field Handbook
- [ ] Camp lantern
- [ ] Camp stove (bottled propane, butane, or white gas) or sterno

stove and extra cans of sterno (never burn charcoal indoors!)

- ☐ Pots/pans
- ☐ Metal cooking spoon
- ☐ Heavy-duty aluminum foil
- ☐ Bottle opener (if appropriate)

- ☐ Dish soap
- ☐ Towel
- ☐ Eye goggles
- ☐ Staple gun
- ☐ Something to read (you may be there a long time)

Other Supplies To Keep in an Accessible Area

Minimum

- ☐ Fireproof box with important papers (including full names and Social Security numbers of all members of family, photographs of family members and pets, vehicle and boat ID numbers and license numbers, insurance policies, charge account numbers, video of valuables/contents of house)
- ☐ Shovel, broom, other cleanup supplies

Also Recommended

- ☐ Plywood, vinyl sheeting
- ☐ Hammer and nails, pliers, screwdrivers
- ☐ Generator (check regulations ahead of time with power company and plan to operate in an open area to ensure good ventilation)

Supplies To Keep in an Evacuation Pack (in case you are asked to leave the neighborhood)

Minimum

- ☐ Backpacks (to put everything else in)
- ☐ Food for 3-5 days (per person) (lightweight ration-type food bars are best)
- ☐ Water (prepackaged in foil pouches or in containers that you can carry)

- ☐ Required prescription medicines and other personal medical supplies
- ☐ First aid kit and handbook
- ☐ Sturdy walking shoes and socks (per person)
- ☐ Jacket (per person)
- ☐ Cash (including coins for telephone)

☐ Social Security numbers of family members

☐ Photographs of family members and pets

☐ Flashlights and extra batteries

☐ Thermal blanket (per person)

☐ Hat (per person)

☐ Sturdy gloves (per older child, adult)

☐ Emergency telephone numbers (including out-of-area contact number)

☐ Portable, battery-operated radio and extra batteries

☐ Keys

Also Recommended _____

☐ Small cooking kit

☐ Extra set of "walk out" clothing

☐ Boy Scout Field Handbook

☐ Premoistened towelettes

☐ Resealable plastic bags and toilet tissue

Supplies To Keep in the Office

☐ Water for 3 days

☐ Food for 3 days (e.g., dried foods, ration-type food bars)

☐ Required prescription medicines for 3 days

☐ Flashlight and extra batteries

☐ Walking shoes and socks

☐ Work gloves

☐ Hat

☐ Backpack

☐ Cash (including coins for telephone)

☐ Battery-operated radio

☐ First aid kit and handbook

☐ Thermal blanket

☐ Emergency telephone numbers (including out-of-area contact number)

☐ Resealable plastic bags and toilet tissue

☐ Jacket/"walk out" clothing

☐ Candles and matches in waterproof container

Supplies To Keep in Your Automobile

Minimum _____

☐ Water for 3 days (per person)

☐ Food for 3 days (per person)

☐ Required prescription medicines for 3 days (per person)

☐ Small first aid kit and handbook

☐ Thermal blanket/blanket

☐ Resealable plastic bags and toilet tissue

☐ Flares

- ☐ Flashlight and extra batteries
- ☐ Car fire extinguisher
- ☐ Sturdy gloves
- ☐ Local maps
- ☐ Notepad and pen/pencil

- ☐ Candles and matches in waterproof container
- ☐ Cash (including coins for telephone)
- ☐ Emergency telephone numbers (including out-of-area contact number)

Also Recommended _____

- ☐ Jumper cables
- ☐ Can of tire puncture seal and inflater
- ☐ Jacket, walking shoes and socks, extra clothing (per person)

- ☐ Compass
- ☐ Something to read

References and Bibliography

Earthquake Preparedness Society. (1989). *Earthquakes & preparedness.* Santa Fe Springs, CA: EPS Downey.

Earthquake safety & survival. (1991). New York: Gordon.

EQE Incorporated. (1987). *Home earthquake preparedness guide.* San Francisco, CA: Author.

Jackson, E. (1991). *Earthquake safety.* Bountiful, UT: Horizon Utah.

Kimball, V. (1992). *Earthquake ready.* Malibu, CA: Roundtable.

Lafferty, L. (1989). *Preparedness guide for earthquakes and other disasters.* La Canada, CA: Lafferty & Associates.

Leach, J. (no date). *Earthquake prepared: Securing your home, protecting your family.* Northridge, CA: Studio 4 Productions.

Nelson, G.M., & Braun, E. (1989). *Earthquake preparedness guide: California edition.* Encino, CA: MXM Imaging.

Quake safe. (1994, February 6). *San Diego Union-Tribune,* pp. H1-H11.

San Diego Home/Garden Lifestyles. (1994). *Earthquake survival guide.* San Diego, CA: McKinnon Enterprises.

Southern California Earthquake Preparedness Project. (1993). *Beat the quake* (assorted materials). Sacramento, CA: Governor's Office of Emergency Services.

Staff. (1994, January 23). On the rebound: Preparing for the next one. *Los Angeles Times,* pp. U11-U12.

Unified San Diego County Emergency Services Organization. (1993). *Earthquake safety checklist.* San Diego, CA: San Diego Gas & Electric.

Wallace, H. (1989). *The Wallace guidebook for emergency care and survival.* Newbury Park, CA: Survivor Industries.

Yanev, P.I. (1990). *Peace of mind in earthquake country* (rev. ed.). San Francisco, CA: Chronicle Books.